Diamonds From Ashes

by Alex Vaune

Chapter One

Broken

i was such a fool
to give my heart
to someone
so careless

-breaking

When we find our own fire
That is when
We become
Truly powerful

-fire

i feel
caught
between two worlds

the dark
and the light

-**caught**

nothing makes me happier
than watching
the sunrise
with
coffee in hand

-**sunrise**

the scars
don't hurt
anymore

but i can't forget
the way
they used to

-scars

cotton candy skies
i close my eyes
and dream

-dream

you are
your own
happy place

-**happy place**

a quiet getaway
is all i need
to get my mind
off of you

-getaway

i love the type of people
who get excited
over starry skies

-my kind of people

we either enter
or leave
this world

broken

-**broken**

the art
of moving on
is making
your heart
finally understand
there's no
turning back

-no turning back

some of us
wander
to find a place

and some of us
wander
to find freedom

-the wanderers

we have so little time
on this earth

but it is enough
if we use it correctly

-time

money will abandon you
but true friends won't

-true value

she was no damsel in distress
she was a dragon
waiting to devour
all who threatened her

-dragon

his love for you
broke you

now let
your love for yourself
heal you

-healing

she was the moon
on a sunny day
hanging in the sky
for not even the sun
could drown out
her beauty

-my moon

you can only reach
a sunny day
by going through
the darkest night

-the sun will rise

as long as you have life
you have hope

-hope

with her
every morning
waking up to her
feels like
christmas morning

-she feels like christmas

you will rise
from your present circumstances
you will survive
you will turn
ashes
into diamonds

-ashes into diamonds

to all the women
who share their stories
of trauma
we applaud your bravery
and thank you
for making our society
a better place

-**bravery**

representation
of women and minorities
in government,
entertainment,
and leadership
is important
full stop.

-representation

is it foolish
to believe
that if we all
loved each other
the best we could
the world would be
a better place?

-**love**

progress
marches on

torches
in the hands
of the downtrodden

let's take
the world
into our own hands

let's create
a better future

-a better future

in the darkest of nights
she reached deep within
and found the most
beautiful hope

-darkest night

her spirit
could crush
ashes
into diamonds

-powerful

Chapter Two

Ashes

she was a flower
they only saw
her petals
but forgot
her thorns

and that's why
they will never expect
her power

-thorns

love is a slow dance
on the moon

-i feel weightless with you

you
are everything
i've ever needed
or wanted

-goddess

i looked up at the stars
and i swear
i caught a glimpse
of your soul

-**stars**

let the rain
wash away
your pain

live a new day
and forget
the pain
of the past

-rain

just the thought
of losing you
is the definition
of pain

-losing you

sing me a lullaby
your voice
gives me life
and sleep

-**your voice**

the world
called her crazy
but they
just didn't understand
her fire

-fire

you looked up at me
on your knees

my gun in your mouth
you begged for death

-oral communication

the world
wanted to destroy her
but they
were no match

for words like dragons breath
power like an ancient king
and a soul
that could put the stars
back in place

-powerful

we are all a bit lost

we just have to find
someone
whose journey
matches our own

-**journey**

how can someone
so broken
be so beautiful?

-her

my idea of heaven
is waking up
next to you
every morning
for the rest
of my life

-**heaven**

i want to trace poetry
on your skin
with my fingers

-**sex**

there is nothing more beautiful
than watching
a woman
become
the ultimate version
of herself

-gasoline on your soul

we learn all the wrong lessons
about love
from people
who don't
understand it

-just do what feels right

everyone else
looked past my flaws

you looked right at them
smiled
and loved all of me

and that's
how i knew
it was real

-love her flaws

i could write
about your love
forever

-forever

a bottle of wine
between us

-**empty**

i would follow you
into the darkness

-follow

with you
life just feels
so simple

and all my problems
just fade away

-**sunshine**

we look
for things
in others

that we wish
we had
ourselves

-law of attraction

don't look for healing
in the same place
you were hurt
in the first place

-healing

Chapter Three

Rising

i am broken
missing you
i wish
i could tape
these wounds closed

-patience

men
are only afraid
of powerful women

-toxic masculinity

you have to love yourself
before
you can love
anyone else

-what comes first

you
are the honey
of my life

a sweet taste
i could never
get off my mind

-sweet nothings

i have no remorse so
beautiful
as loving you

-remorse

don't be ashamed
of feeling hurt

life hurts
that's part of it

-tears

you
are a beautiful flower
just waiting
to bloom

such beautiful potential

bloom, my darling, bloom

-bloom

loving someone
is like shooting a bullet
at a glass sculpture

-good things hurt the most

it sucks to realize
how many people
don't even notice
when you disappear

-tragedy of solitude

she told me
she takes it as a compliment
when men
call her a bitch

it means
they're offended
by her power

-bitch

broken people
love the deepest

-deep

don't worry about death
worry about truly living
while you still can

-living

it's such a tragedy
to waste the present
thinking about mistakes
from the past

let them go
be free

-let go

if someone doesn't care
about you

don't give them
the time of day

they aren't worth
your time and effort

-time & effort

you deserve someone
who fights for you
and wants to be with you
all the time
not just when it's easy

-you deserve to be fought for

my idea of perfect
begins
and ends
with you

-perfect

when you're sad
remember
that it makes
the happy moments
feel
even happier

-sad

with sad eyes
i look at our old photos
our precious memories

-**missing you**

always trust
your gut

it knows what you want
before your mind does

-trust your gut

love and hate
are two sides
of the same coin

the higher you fly
the harder you fall
and the more it hurts
in the end

-in the end

poetry is...

-whatever you make it

every picture of me
feels like
it's missing something
without you

-ghost

make amends
with those who hurt you

it's the hardest thing
but the most worth it

-forgiveness

she was the aurora borealis
lighting up
the darkest nights
with her beauty

-aurora borealis

he left you broken
but
you
are strong enough
to pick up
the pieces

-broken

overthinking
is a hazardous habit

-overthinking

the hardest part
is at the end

wondering
if they ever
really loved you
at all

-post mortem

fuck average compliments

tell her she's kind
before calling her beautiful

tell her she's special
before calling her sexy

human beings are not objects
you must know the heart
before you know the body

-compliments

stop giving effort
to people
who don't care
about you

-equal effort

being angry at someone
doesn't hurt them
it just hurts you

turn your eyes
to the light
and let yourself
begin to heal

-turn your eyes to the light

falling down
doesn't mean
you're losing

unless
you stay down

-get back up

you were the vice
i could never get rid of

-vice

never forget
that you have the power
to be the person
you want to be

-the power to change

ask yourself:

what would i be doing right now
if i could do anything?

what would i do right now
if i had no fear?

then set your sights
on those goals
and make them happen

-happy life

the most powerful force
in the universe
is a person
who can look
deep within themselves
and find the strength
to keep going

-against all odds

what do you like
about yourself?

focus on that

and everything else
will follow

-focus on the positive

the strongest glue
between any two people
is forgiveness

-hold me together

don't look
for someone else
to make you happy

make yourself happy
and look for someone
to share happiness with

-sharing

laughter
is the beginning
of healing

it is the first ray
of sunshine
to reach the sunflower

-sunflower

true love
is in your reach

you only have to look
inwards

-love yourself first and foremost

anger
fear
sadness
jealousy
pain

these are all
negative frequencies

you must let them go
and pursue positive frequencies
to feel free
and begin to heal

-frequencies & vibes

live your own life

don't live
how the world
expects you to

the only path
towards happiness
is pursuing the paths
your soul contained
since before you were born

-follow your destiny

no one ever succeeded
without first failing

don't be discouraged
by the difficulty
of the moment

it will pass
as all seasons do

-seasons

in your loneliest times
remember
to be there
first and foremost
for yourself

-be there for yourself

no one ever accomplished anything
by believing they couldn't

success
starts in the mind.

-mentality

the same legs that stumbled
will let you get up

-always get up

never forget
that thinking
about the past
takes away
from the present moment

forget the past
live in the now

-live now

you are never a burden
you
are never difficult to love

you are beautiful
you are joy
you are perfect
and you
are not
what they label you as

-labels

thank you for reading

-Alex Vaune

Made in the USA
Middletown, DE
28 January 2018